BOMB SQUAD TECHNICIANS
IN ACTION

BY ROBERTA BAXTER

The Child's World®
childsworld.com

Published by The Child's World®
1980 Lookout Drive • Mankato, MN 56003-1705
800-599-READ • www.childsworld.com

Photographs ©: Milan Tomazin/Shutterstock Images, cover, 1;
Cpl. Paul S. Martinez/U.S. Marine Corps, 5; iStockphoto, 6; Leonard
Zhukovsky/Shutterstock Images, 8; Ken Klotzbach/Post-Bulletin/AP Images,
10; Shutterstock Images, 11, 18; Cpl. Levi Schultz/U.S. Marine Corps, 12;
Sgt. Owen Kimbrel/U.S. Marine Corps, 14; Mass Communication Specialist
1st Class Daniel R. Mennuto/U.S. Navy, 15; Patrick A. Albright/U.S. Army,
16; Henny Ray Abrams/AP Images, 21; Mark Lennihan/AP Images, 22;
Marcio Jose Bastos Silva/Shutterstock Images, 24; Charles Krupa/AP Images,
26; Federal Bureau of Investigation, 27, 28

ISBN 9781503816275

LCCN 2016945857

Printed in the United States of America
PA02320

TABLE OF
CONTENTS

FAST FACTS

What's the Job?

- Bomb squad technicians locate explosive devices. They find out what kind of devices they are and how they are wired.

- Technicians make the devices safe or destroy them.

- Some bomb squad technicians work in the military. Others work in law enforcement.

- Training is done by the military. It is also done at the Hazardous Devices School in Alabama.

The Dangers

- Technicians can be seriously injured by explosive devices.

- In some cases, technicians have died.

Important Stats

- Law enforcement bomb squad technicians usually earn between $50,000 and $80,000 a year.

- Most military members earn between $21,000 and $35,000 a year. However, bomb squad members earn large bonuses on top of their base salaries.

- Experts expect the field to grow approximately 5 percent through 2022.

Chapter 1

TRAINING TO BE AN EXPERT

On a U.S. Army post in Alabama, there are 14 towns. The towns are part of a training facility. Each town is filled with hidden explosives. The explosives could be in the movie theater. They could be in a store. Or maybe they are hidden in a parked car.

A bomb disposal technician slides on an ice vest. This vest will help her body stay cool in the Alabama heat. Then she pulls on the rest of her 90-pound (41-kg) suit. The weight feels like 10 gallons of milk hanging from her body.

An air tank is strapped on her back. A helmet is clamped down on her head. The helmet alone weighs 15 pounds (7 kg). It has lights and a defogger. It also has a fan. The bomb squad technician does not wear anything on her hands. She needs her fingers free. This helps her work easily in tight spaces.

The only thing the technician can hear now is her own heart. Then she notices the hiss of the **respirator** bringing her air.

◀ **Bomb disposal technicians wear heavy suits to protect themselves from blasts.**

▲ **Bomb squads often use robots to do the most dangerous jobs.**

She clears her mind of everything except the job. She takes deep breaths to calm herself.

The technician picks up her bag of tools. It contains pliers, screwdrivers, drill bits, and flashlights. The bag also includes a portable X-ray machine. She enters one of the tiny towns. On the first street, she notices a parked car.

She pulls a tool out of her bag. It's a metal rod with a mirror attached to one end. She uses the tool to scan the bottom of the car. There's no bomb underneath. Next she checks the inside of the car. Then she carefully opens the trunk. She checks for wires that might **detonate** a bomb. The car is clear of explosives. The technician moves on to the town's bookstore.

She checks under the sales counter. She looks around the bookshelves. She spots no explosive devices, so she moves to the next store. She peers under a table in a coffee shop. There she finds a suspicious package. The technician takes a joystick from her bag. She uses the joystick to drive a robot near the package. For safety, the technician crouches down behind a nearby wall. She uses the robot's camera to guide its front claw.

With the joystick, the technician makes the robot grasp the package. Then she rolls the robot back. The robot places the package in a **containment vessel**. Later, the suspicious package will be detonated inside the containment vessel.

In an alley, the technician finds another bomb. This one is stuck to the side of an electrical box. She can't remove the bomb by herself. So, she uses the robot again. This time she directs the robot to shoot a blast of water at the device. The water travels at the speed of a bullet. It destroys the wiring and the heart of the bomb.

▲ **Containment vessels are often carried on trailers or small carts.**

The technician pulls off her helmet. She breathes a sigh of relief. The exercise is over. Now she can return to the classroom and learn more. She is a student at the Hazardous Devices School. The school is operated by the U.S. Army and the Federal Bureau of Investigation (FBI). The school opened in 1971.

It has trained more than 18,000 bomb disposal technicians for law enforcement jobs.

The bomb-filled towns really exist, but no people live there. Students gain valuable knowledge and skills by practicing in these towns. When the students are ready, they face actual bomb situations. Then, after graduating, students move to different cities. They become members of bomb squads.

▲ **A bomb squad technician uses a long pole to place a suspicious bag into a containment vessel.**

Chapter 2

MILITARY EOD

In October 2013, a team of U.S. Army Rangers attacked an enemy compound in Afghanistan. One of the enemy fighters began to flee. A group of American soldiers chased him. Suddenly, explosions rang out. The compound was full of improvised explosive devices (IEDs). IEDs are homemade bombs. They can be packed with nails or metal fragments. These fragments fly out when the bomb explodes. The IEDs can be detonated by walking on them. They can also be detonated by using a cell phone to send a signal to the bomb. IEDs can be small pipe bombs. Or they can be larger bombs that explode a car.

Staff Sergeant Jeffery Dawson was with the team. Jeffery was an explosive **ordnance** disposal (EOD) specialist. His job was to find and disarm the IEDs. Bomb squad technicians have the mission of locating explosive devices and disarming or disabling them. Their actions save their own lives. They also save the lives of fellow members of the military.

◄ **An EOD technician uses a metal detector to look for explosives.**

▲ **An EOD technician changes the batteries of a robot.**

Jeffery thought back to all of his training. First he had finished basic training. Then he had attended advanced training for his career in bomb disposal. Each military branch has its own qualifications and training for EOD technicians.

Recruits for this field must receive high technical scores on the Armed Services Vocational Aptitude Battery Test (ASVAB). People who want to enlist in the military take this exam.

▲ An EOD technician practices handling explosives during a training exercise.

▲ **Staff Sergeant Jeffery Dawson (left) receives a Distinguished Service Cross.**

EOD candidates must be in top physical condition. They must have good eyesight. They also need to be comfortable working in tight spaces.

Jeffery began searching for a path through the bombs. This path would allow a medic to reach the wounded soldiers. From his position, Jeffery could see six or seven IEDs. The IEDs looked like little anthills. He began to mark them. That way, other soldiers could pass through safely.

In the distance, Jeffery heard the sound of a helicopter. The rescue team was on its way. But as the helicopter hovered overhead, more devices exploded. They had been set off by the pressure of the helicopter's movement.

Using his metal detector, Jeffery continued to find and mark the explosives. But another IED detonated before he could mark it. The blast knocked him off his feet. Fragments of metal tore into his leg. Jeffery was wounded, but he kept working. He said he was following his EOD training. Jeffery knew he had to find the IEDs to keep as many people safe as possible.

In time, more EOD specialists arrived. Jeffery told them where he had marked IEDs. He also pointed out the areas that had not yet been cleared. Then he got into a helicopter. The pilot flew him to an American base for medical attention. Months later, Jeffery received one of the U.S. Army's highest awards for his bravery and skill.

Chapter 3

LAW ENFORCEMENT BOMB SQUAD

In January 2015, police officers were called to a shopping center in Lodi, California. The officers were there to arrest a woman. She was accused of shoplifting. The police found her in the parking lot. Then the officers saw two suspicious packages on the seat of her car. They immediately called the local bomb squad.

The bomb squad soon arrived on the scene. They decided that both devices needed to be **defused**. The first device was a pipe bomb. Using a robot, a bomb squad officer set off a small explosive to disarm the first bomb. The other device was meant to make a large fireball. Technicians used the robot to shoot a water blast. This blast disabled the second bomb.

Sergeant Steve Maynard was on the scene. He said both bombs could have caused major damage if they had detonated.

◀ **Pipe bombs are homemade explosives that can be set off by electronic devices.**

Fortunately, the bombs had been discovered before they could hurt anyone or destroy property.

The bomb squad receives many calls that turn out to be nothing dangerous. In November 2015, a bus driver in West Haven, Connecticut, noticed an abandoned suitcase. He sent the passengers off of his bus. Then he called the police. The bomb squad quickly arrived. They investigated the suitcase and found that it was full of clothes. Someone had simply forgotten it.

Like Lodi and West Haven, most medium-sized cities have a bomb squad. Usually people work on the squad part-time. Bomb squad team members work as regular police officers until they get a call for a possible bomb.

Large cities usually have full-time bomb squads to call in when needed. In May 2010, a T-shirt vendor in New York City noticed something strange. An **SUV** was parked crookedly near Times Square. Smoke was coming out of the vents near the back seat of the vehicle. The vendor reported the incident to a police officer. When the officer investigated, he smelled gunpowder. He called for the bomb squad. Then he began sending people out of the area.

The SUV was still running. A firefighter arrived on the scene early. He heard pops inside the vehicle. No one knew what to expect.

While all the people in Times Square were leaving, the bomb squad arrived. The squad members put on their suits. They hooked up the joystick for the robot. One bomb squad technician made the robot roll forward until it was even with the SUV. He made the robot break a window in the vehicle. The technician knew this action might cause the car to explode. It didn't, so he used the robot's camera to look inside.

▲ **Video surveillance footage shows a bomb-filled SUV in Times Square.**

▲ **A bomb squad technician puts on his suit in Times Square.**

He saw three propane bottles, similar to those used on a backyard grill. There were also cans of gasoline, fireworks, and two clocks. This vehicle was carrying a homemade bomb.

Some of the fireworks had gone off. They had caused the pops that the firefighter heard. But the fireworks had not detonated the explosive device. Bomb squad technicians were able to separate the parts of the unsuccessful bomb. If the car bomb had gone off, it would have exploded into a large fireball. Many people could have been hurt or killed.

Like most law enforcement bomb squad technicians, members of the New York City squad trained at the Hazardous Devices School in Alabama. One of the bombs that students must defuse at the school is similar to the one built by the Times Square bomber. The New York City bomb squad members remembered their training when it mattered most.

Sometimes bomb squads are called into action when a person finds unexploded grenades or bombs. In 2015, a group of kids found an old bomb in a wildlife refuge near Portland, Oregon. They should not have touched the bomb, but they carried it home. An adult at home realized that the kids had brought home a bomb. The adult immediately called the police.

When the police arrived, they cleared out neighboring homes. Bomb squad technicians from the local law enforcement unit and from the nearby Air National Guard EOD team removed the bomb. Fortunately, they were able to detonate it in a safe place.

Chapter 4

THE FBI'S BOMB LIBRARY

On April 15, 2013, a police bomb squad scanned the streets of Boston, Massachusetts. Thousands of runners and spectators were in town for the 117th annual Boston Marathon. The bomb squad was on high alert. They knew the event's popularity could make it a target for a terrorist attack.

Bomb technician Mitch McCormick stood near the finish line. At about 2:50 p.m., he heard a loud boom. He thought it might be someone shooting off a celebratory cannon. But a second booming sound followed. He felt the vibrations in his chest. He then knew with certainty the sources of the sounds. They were bombs.

Mitch ran through the streets. He searched for bomb fragments. Discarded shoes, jackets, and water bottles littered the ground. But then he found a twisted piece of sheet metal. He also found a battery. He recognized these as parts of a bomb.

◀ **The Boston Marathon is the world's oldest annual marathon.**

▲ **Rescue workers help victims after the bombing.**

The Boston bomb squad gathered the bomb fragments. They identified these as parts of two pipe bombs. The bombs had killed three people. More than 260 were injured. The bombers had fled. But the bomb technicians hoped the fragments would offer enough clues to figure out who was responsible.

The bomb parts were sent to the FBI's Terrorist Explosive Device Analytical Center (TEDAC) in Virginia. This "bomb library" houses bomb parts from all over the world. Bomb technicians, scientists, and engineers study them. Each bomb part has a bomber's "signature." This could be fingerprints or DNA. But the way a bomb is made also provides clues about who made it.

TEDAC technicians examined the Boston Marathon bomb fragments. The bombs contained parts from Christmas lights and model cars. Technicians could not recover many fingerprints. But they tried to find out where these items had been purchased and who had purchased them.

▲ **A technician examines a pipe bomb at the Terrorist Explosive Device Analytical Center.**

▲ **A TEDAC technician takes photographs of an explosive device.**

A few days after the bombing, two men shot and killed a police officer in the nearby city of Cambridge, Massachusetts. They then stole a car and took its driver **hostage**. The hostage managed to escape. He called the police from a gas station. He described how one of the men had pointed a gun at him. The man said that he was one of the Boston Marathon bombers.

Police chased the stolen car. The two men started shooting. They also began throwing pipe bombs. The shootout lasted 20 hours.

One of the suspects died during the shootout. But the other survived. Bomb technicians studied pieces of the bombs the suspects had thrown. These bombs matched the Boston Marathon pipe bombs. The fingerprints on some of the Boston Marathon bomb fragments matched the suspects' fingerprints. Thanks to the work of TEDAC technicians, the mystery of the Boston Marathon bombers was solved. The surviving bomber was brought to justice.

Bomb technicians sometimes work on the front lines and defuse bombs. Others, such as the TEDAC technicians, work behind the scenes in labs. No matter where they work, bomb technicians use their skills to keep others safe.

THINK ABOUT IT

- What personal characteristics would be most important for a bomb squad technician? Why?
- What would be the hardest thing to do if you were a bomb squad technician?
- Can you think of a way to make the job of bomb squad technician safer?

GLOSSARY

containment vessel (kun-TAYN-ment VEH-suhl): A containment vessel is a heavy metal can that holds in the blast of a bomb. The robot placed the bomb in a containment vessel so that the bomb would not harm anyone.

defused (dee-FYOOZD): Defused means made something harmless so it would not explode. The bomb squad technician defused the bomb by cutting a wire.

detonate (DEH-tun-ayt): Detonate means to explode. The bomb will detonate when the timer goes off.

hostage (HAHS-tij): A hostage is someone who is captured by a person demanding certain things. The robber said he would not release the hostage unless he received money.

ordnance (ORD-nens): Ordnance is military weapons or ammunition. The unexploded ordnance was dangerous.

respirator (RES-pur-ay-tur): A respirator is a device with a mask that helps a person breathe air from a tank. The bomb squad technician breathed through a respirator.

SUV: An SUV is a sport utility vehicle, which is a vehicle that has lots of storage space and four-wheel drive. A bomber in Times Square filled an SUV with explosives.

TO LEARN MORE

Books

Fitzgerald, Lee. *Bomb Squads*. New York: PowerKids Press, 2016.

Gordon, Nick. *Bomb Squad Technician*. Minneapolis: Bellwether Media, 2013.

Perritano, John. *Bomb Squad Technician*. Broomall, PA: Mason Crest, 2015.

Web Sites

Visit our Web site for links about bomb squad technicians: childsworld.com/links

Note to Parents, Teachers, and Librarians: We routinely verify our Web links to make sure they are safe and active sites. So encourage your readers to check them out!

SELECTED BIBLIOGRAPHY

Baker, Al, and William K. Rashbaum. "Police Find Car Bomb in Times Square." *New York Times*. New York Times Company, 1 May 2010. Web. 23 May 2016.

Esposito, Richard, and Ted Gerstein. *Bomb Squad: A Year Inside the Nation's Most Exclusive Police Unit*. New York: Hyperion, 2007. Print.

Tan, Michelle. "Soldiers Receive Distinguished Service Cross for Incredible Valor." *Army Times*. Armytimes.com, 17 Feb. 2015. Web. 23 May 2016.

INDEX

ABOUT THE AUTHOR

Roberta Baxter has written more than 30 books about science and history for students of all ages. She knows and admires people who work in dangerous jobs, such as bomb squad technicians.